THE SUPERTEAMS

MAN UTD

ALL EVERY UNITED FAN NEEDS TO KNOW ABOUT THE 1998/99 SEASON

MANCHESTER UNITED MANCHESTER UNITED MANCHESTER
TED MANCHESTER UNITED MANCHESTER UNITED MANCHESTER UNITE
NCHESTER UNITED MANCHESTER UNITED MANCHESTER UNITE
TED MANCHESTER UNITED MANCHESTER UNITED MANCHESTER UNITE
NCHESTER UNITED MANCHESTER UNITED MANCHESTER UNITE
TED MANCHESTER UNITED MANCHESTER UNITED MANCHESTER UNITE
NCHESTER UNITED MANCHESTER UNITED MANCHESTER UNITE
TED MANCHESTER UNITED MANCHESTER UNITED MANCHESTER UNITE
NCHESTER UNITED MANCHESTER UNITED MANCHESTER UNITE
TED MANCHESTER UNITED MANCHESTER UNITED MANCHESTER UNITE
NCHESTER UNITED MANCHESTER UNITED MANCHESTER UNITE
TED MANCHESTER UNITED MANCHESTER UNITED MANCHESTER UNITE
NCHESTER UNITED MANCHESTER UNITED MANCHESTER UNITE
TED MANCHESTER UNITED MANCHESTER UNITED MANCHESTER UNITE
NCHESTER UNITED MANCHESTER UNITED MANCHESTER UNITE
TED MANCHESTER UNITED MANCHESTER UNITED MANCHESTER UNITE
NCHESTER UNITED MANCHESTER UNITED MANCHESTER UNITE
TED MANCHESTER UNITED MANCHESTER UNITED MANCHESTER UNITE
NCHESTER UNITED MANCHESTER UNITED MANCHESTER UNITE
TED MANCHESTER UNITED MANCHESTER UNITED MANCHESTER UNITE
NCHESTER UNITED MANCHESTER UNITED MANCHESTER UNITE
TED MANCHESTER UNITED MANCHESTER UNITED MANCHESTER UNITE
NCHESTER UNITED MANCHESTER UNITED MANCHESTER UNITE
TED MANCHESTER UNITED MANCHESTER UNITED MANCHESTER UNITE
NCHESTER UNITED MANCHESTER UNITED MANCHESTER UNITE
TED MANCHESTER UNITED MANCHESTER UNITED MANCHESTER UNITE
NCHESTER UNITED MANCHESTER UNITED MANCHESTER UNITE

mustard

TED MANCHESTER UNITED MANCHESTER UNITED MANCHESTER UNITE
NCHESTER UNITED MANCHESTER UNITED MANCHESTER UNITE
TED MANCHESTER UNITED MANCHESTER UNITED MANCHESTER UNITE
NCHESTER UNITED MANCHESTER UNITED MANCHESTER UNITE

First published in 1999 by Mustard

Mustard is an imprint of Parragon

**Parragon
Queen Street House
4 Queen Street
Bath BA1 1HE, UK**

British Library Cataloguing-in Publication Data.

A catalogue record for this book is available
from the British Library.

ISBN 1 84164 249 5

Printed in Italy

CONTENTS

Up For It!

1998 was a disappointment, with United failing to win a trophy – but 1999 was going to be different for **Alex Ferguson** and his team. Different enough for the Scotsman to be voted **Manager of the Year** after his team won... but that would be telling. Here are the players he had at his disposal.

DEFENCE

The big summer signing was Dutchman **Jaap Stam**, joining such established stars as **Gary** and **Phil Neville**, **Denis Irwin**, **Henning Berg** and **Ronnie Johnsen** in front of goalkeeping legend, **Peter Schmeichel**, or occasionally **Raimond van der Gouw**.

MIDFIELD

One man with a lot to prove after his red card in England's World Cup campaign was **David Beckham**, while back soon into the season after nearly a year out with injury was **Roy Keane**. The rest of the talent was equally impressive: **Ryan Giggs**, **Nicky Butt**, **Paul Scholes** and new Swedish signing **Jesper Blomqvist**.

ATTACK

At the start of the season, the star strikers were England's **Andy Cole**

KICK-OFF

and **Teddy Sheringham** and Norwegian **Ole Gunnar Solskjaer**. But Alex Ferguson had set his sights on signing another player, and eventually **Dwight Yorke** from Trinidad & Tobago was prised away from Aston Villa to create the deadliest collection of strikers in the Premiership.

IN THE HOT SEAT

Alex Ferguson took over as Manchester United manager in December 1986 after a successful career in Scotland in charge of **Aberdeen**, winning several trophies including the 1983 European Cup-Winners' Cup.

The Glory

The season started with two priorities: to get back that Premiership title and win the European Cup. So United could afford to ignore the Charity Shield – though it marked the return of **Roy Keane** to the first team after ten months out through injury. Beating Polish side **LKS Lodz** was what mattered, and that was done easily enough. In the league, Leicester City led 2-0 at Old Trafford on the opening day

Roy is back!

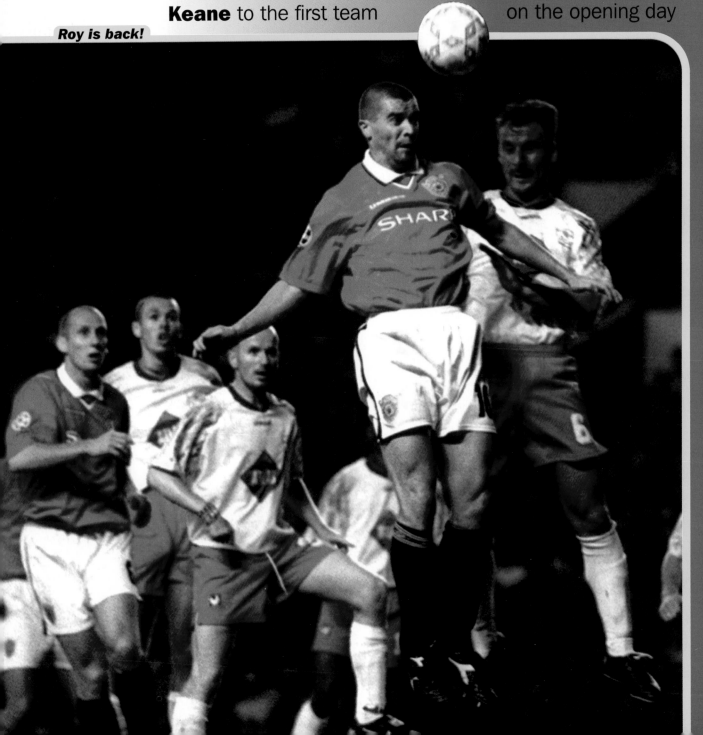

before Teddy Sheringham and a **David Beckham free kick special** won a point, getting back at his critics. Then came the big news of the month: the £12.6m signing of **Dwight Yorke** from Aston Villa in time to start against West Ham.

" You saw the **measure of the guy** out there "

LEICESTER'S NEIL LENNON on David Beckham's gutsy showing

STATS

PREMIER LEAGUE

Leicester City	D	2-2	Sheringham Beckham
West Ham	D	0-0	

CHAMPIONS LEAGUE

LKS Lodz	W	2-0	Giggs, Cole
(2nd Preliminary Round, 1st Leg)			
LKS Lodz	D	0-0	
(2nd Preliminary Round, 2nd Leg)			

Manchester United win 2-0 on aggregate

CHARITY SHIELD

Arsenal	L	0-3	
(Wembley)			

DID YOU KNOW?

Manchester United may have lost the Charity Shield this season, but they have won it outright **more times than any other team**. United have ten wins, with Arsenal next best on eight.

Ryan lets fly

Eurovisions

Two great performances in Europe as the **Champions League** proper started, but the games ended in two draws rather than two wins. **Barcelona** were 2-0 down at half time, but got two penalties to leave Alex Ferguson fuming and drew 3-3, in spite of another **great Beckham free kick**. Then Bayern Munich equalised twice, once through an offside goal, then in the last minute from a rare mistake by Peter Schmeichel. In the league, only Arsenal posed any problems, though it was a third straight win for them in the league against United. But a 2-0 defeat at Old Trafford did its bit to expose **Liverpool** once again.

SEPTEMBER

> **After the game I saw the Barcelona president go into the referee's dressing room. He certainly had cause to be happy with him**

ALEX FERGUSON, **unhappy with the decisions that cost United**

STATS

PREMIER LEAGUE

Charlton	W	4-1	Solskjaer (2) Yorke (2)
Coventry	W	2-0	Yorke, Johnsen
Arsenal	L	0-3	
Liverpool	W	2-0	Irwin (pen) Scholes

CHAMPIONS LEAGUE

Barcelona (Group D)	D	3-3	Giggs, Scholes Beckham
Bayern Munich (Group D)	D	2-2	Yorke, Scholes

Good day's work

DID YOU KNOW?

The win over Liverpool confirmed United's superiority from the start and this would be **the eighth straight year** Alex Ferguson's team finished ahead of their so-called rivals.

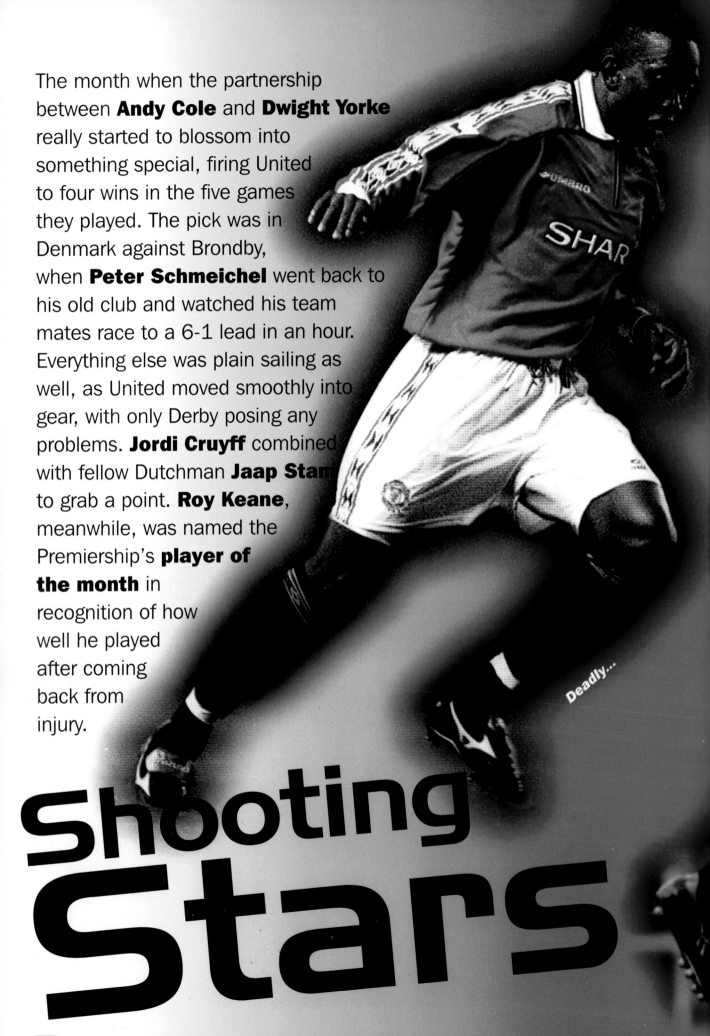

The month when the partnership between **Andy Cole** and **Dwight Yorke** really started to blossom into something special, firing United to four wins in the five games they played. The pick was in Denmark against Brondby, when **Peter Schmeichel** went back to his old club and watched his team mates race to a 6-1 lead in an hour. Everything else was plain sailing as well, as United moved smoothly into gear, with only Derby posing any problems. **Jordi Cruyff** combined with fellow Dutchman **Jaap Stam** to grab a point. **Roy Keane**, meanwhile, was named the Premiership's **player of the month** in recognition of how well he played after coming back from injury.

Deadly...

Shooting Stars

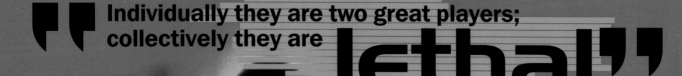

OCTOBER

"Individually they are two great players; collectively they are **lethal**"

WIMBLEDON'S KENNY CUNNINGHAM
on Yorke and Cole after the 5-1 win

DID YOU KNOW?

When Division One club Bury lost at Old Trafford in the Worthington Cup, there was one spectator with divided loyalties. **Neville Neville**, the improbably named father of United stars **Gary** and **Phil**, is commercial manager of Bury.

.duo
.oup

STATS

PREMIER LEAGUE

Southampton	W 3-0	Yorke, Cole, Cruyff
Wimbledon	W 5-1	Cole (2), Giggs, Beckham, Yorke
Derby	D 1-1	Cruyff
Everton	W 4-1	Yorke, Short (o.g.), Cole, Blomqvist

CHAMPIONS LEAGUE

Brondby	W 6-2	Giggs (2), Cole, Keane
(Group D)		Yorke, Solskjaer

WORTHINGTON CUP

Bury	W 2-0	Solskjaer, Nevland
(3rd Round)		

Fire Power

" **If we can finish this year by**

winning the Champions League

that would be tremendous for me and also for the club. "

PETER SCHMEICHEL names his parting ambition as he announces his retirement

Poor old Brondby. United were way too good for the Danes, scoring five in an hour to knock them out of **Champions League** contention. The Reds then went to **Barcelona** and did the same, in a match every bit as thrilling as the one at Old Trafford – and with the same scoreline. The Spanish side had to win but were powerless against United's lightning breaks, with **Cole** and **Yorke** outstanding. In the league, United kept in touch with the leaders with two narrow wins and a draw, though one game was lost. Meanwhile, **Ole Gunnar Solskjaer** got a rare full game against Nottingham Forest in the Worthington Cup, scoring twice.

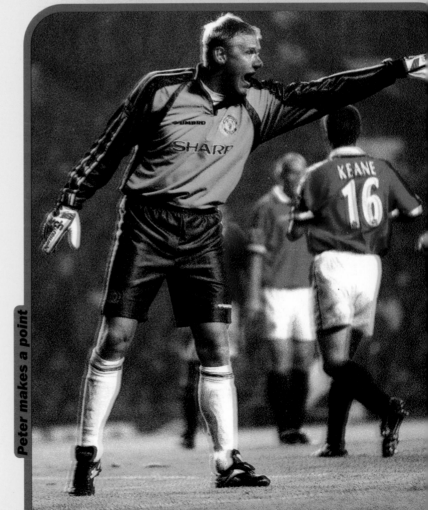

Peter makes a point

NOVEMBER

Roy's bagged it

DID YOU KNOW?

United scored **eight goals** in Champions League matches this month on their way to becoming **the highest scorers** in the group stages this season.

PREMIER LEAGUE

Newcastle Utd	D	0-0	
Blackburn	W	3-2	Scoles (2), Yorke
Sheffield Wed	L	1-3	Cole
Leeds Utd	W	3-2	Solskjaer, Keane, Butt

CHAMPIONS LEAGUE

Brondby (Group D)	W	5-0	Beckham, Cole, P Neville, Yorke, Scholes
Barcelona (Group D)	D	3-3	Yorke (2), Scholes

WORTHINGTON CUP

Nottingham F (4th Round)	W	2-1	Solskjaer (2)

Steady Pace

DID YOU KNOW?

Since the Champions League started, Manchester United are **the only English team to reach the knockout stages** – and they've done it for each of the last three years.

Take a breather

DECEMBER

> "We are not scared of any of the remaining teams. There's a lot **more to come** from us yet"

ROY KEANE after the draw with Munich saw United through in the Champions League

As **Bayern Munich** came to Old Trafford, a draw would probably be enough for both sides to advance in the Champions League – and that's what happened. **Roy Keane** gave the Reds the lead, but **Salihamidzic** equalised and both sides advanced to the quarter-finals. The draw paired United with **Inter Milan**. In fact, **draw** was the key word of December, with four of them in the league, including two against title rivals Chelsea. Losing to Spurs in the Worthington Cup didn't really matter, but it did hurt when old boy **Bryan Robson** brought his Middlesbrough team to Old Trafford and won. **Alex Ferguson** was away for family reasons and though the team came back from 3-0 down they couldn't quite make it in his absence.

Take Jaap!

STATS

PREMIER LEAGUE

Aston Villa	D	1-1	Scholes
Tottenham	D	2-2	Solskjaer (2)
Chelsea	D	1-1	Cole
Middlesbrough	L	2-3	Butt, Scholes
Nottingham F	W	3-0	Johnsen (2)
			Giggs
Chelsea	D	0-0	

CHAMPIONS LEAGUE

Bayern Munich	D	1-1	Keane
(Group D)			

WORTHINGTON CUP

Tottenham	L	1-3	Sheringham
(5th Round)			

Awesome!

You can't do better than five games, five wins. In the FA Cup, there was quick revenge over **Middlesbrough** for December's league defeat, followed by a tremendous win over old rivals **Liverpool**. Trailing for 85 minutes until Andy Cole set up **Dwight Yorke** from a Beckham free kick, United then won the game in injury time through **supersub Ole Gunnar Solskjaer**. In the league, Yorke and Cole were on fire against West Ham and Leicester.

Then it was another last-minute effort that beat Charlton at The Valley to complete a perfect month. On top of that, **Dwight Yorke** was named the Premiership's **player of the month**, and **Alex Ferguson** was named **manager of the month**.

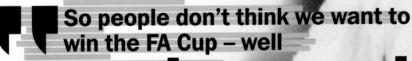

So people don't think we want to win the FA Cup – well **we showed differently** out there!

FERGUSON after beating Liverpool

that famous smile

Airborne

STATS

PREMIER LEAGUE

West Ham	W 4-1	Yorke, Cole (2) Solskjaer
Leicester City	W 6-2	Yorke (3), Cole (2) Stam
Charlton	W 1-0	Yorke

FA CUP

Middlesbrough (3rd Round)	W 3-1	Cole, Irwin (pen) Giggs
Liverpool (4th Round)	W 2-1	Yorke, Solskjaer

DID YOU KNOW?

Liverpool haven't beaten United at Old Trafford since 1990, and **haven't even won at home** since 1995!

Fourwards!

Alex keeps count

So he was Supersub in January – but what do you call **Ole Gunnar Solskjaer** after he tore Nottingham Forest apart with **four goals in 14 minutes**? The 8-1 demolition was the highlight of **another unbeaten month** with only Arsenal getting anything out of a game with the Reds. Forest are managed by Ron Atkinson, the manager of United before **Alex Ferguson** took over 13 years ago.

The only points dropped were to Arsenal, after **Dwight Yorke** missed a penalty. Though with all the wins apart from Forest being a single goal, it might have been better if those **eight goals** had been spread around a bit!

STATS

PREMIER LEAGUE

Derby County	W 1-0	Yorke	
Nottingham F	W 8-1	Yorke (2)	
		Cole (2)	
		Solskjaer (4)	
Arsenal	D 1-1	Cole	
Coventry City	W 1-0	Giggs	
Southampton	W 2-1	Keane, Yorke	

FA CUP

Fulham	W 1-0	Cole	
(5th Round)			

DID YOU KNOW?

Ole Gunnar Solskjaer turned down a **move to Tottenham** early in the season because **he'd rather play for United from the bench** than start for another Premiership team!

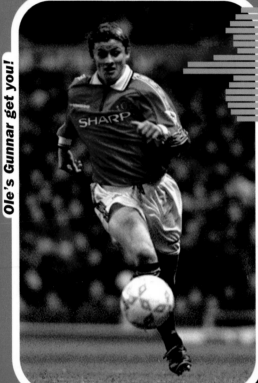

Ole's Gunnar get you!

> **"In a nutshell, we got**
> # murdered
> **Former boss *RON ATKINSON* after his Forest team lost 8-1 "**

Bundle!

Unbeaten once more – and the only draws came in the Cups, with United winning the ties. In the league, **Andy Cole went back to Newcastle** and won the game, and Everton were dealt with easily enough. But the real drama came elsewhere. **Two magnificent Beckham crosses** and two great Yorke headers beat Inter Milan at Old Trafford in the Champions League quarter-finals, and **Paul Scholes made things safe** late on in the return leg. Chelsea might have fancied their chances in the FA Cup after drawing at Old Trafford, but **a magnificent chip** by Yorke after strong work by Cole sealed a 2-0 win at Stamford Bridge. Suddenly, **talk of an historic treble** was everywhere.

Two for Andy

Measuring up

Treble

> ## "Jaap is a **quality player**
> ### and he did a great job on Alan. But then Jaap's been doing a great job all season "

ANDY COLE on Jaap Stam after the win over Newcastle United

STATS

PREMIER LEAGUE

Newcastle Utd	W 2-1	Cole (2)
Everton	W 3-1	Solskjaer,
		G Neville
		Beckham

CHAMPIONS LEAGUE

Inter Milan	W 2-0	Yorke (2)

(Quarter-Final, 1st Leg)

Inter Milan	D 1-1	Scholes

*(Quarter-Final, 2nd Leg – **Manchester United win 3-1 on aggregate**)*

FA CUP

Chelsea	D 0-0	

(Quarter-Final)

Chelsea	W 2-0	Yorke (2)

(Quarter-Final Replay)

Chance

DID YOU KNOW?

When United beat Inter Milan in the Champions League, it was the **first time** they had ever **knocked out an Italian side** in European competition. They didn't have to wait long to do it again...

Comeback

What a month! What a goal! What a comeback! Where to begin? **Ryan Giggs** struck twice, crucially, to keep both Cup dreams alive. A last-minute equaliser at Old Trafford against Juventus gave United hope for the second leg. At 2-0 down it looked all over. But the team rallied, and Andy Cole sealed the 3-2 win that meant **a return to the European Cup Final** after 31 years. Then **Giggs** won the FA Cup Semi-Final replay against Arsenal with an **amazing goal**, running from his own half as ten-man United reached Wembley. **Peter Schmeichel** had saved a last-minute **penalty** to take the game to extra time; only a wrongly-disallowed Roy Keane goal had led to the replay, so **justice was done**. Still top of the league in spite of two draws – the treble was on! No surprise **Fergie** was again **manager of the month**.

Come on, Ref!

STATS

PREMIER LEAGUE

Wimbledon	D	1-1	Beckham
Sheffield Wed	W	3-0	Solskjaer
			Sheringham
			Scholes
Leeds United	D	1-1	Cole

CHAMPIONS LEAGUE

Juventus	D	1-1	Giggs

(Semi-Final, 1st Leg)

Juventus	W	3-2	Keane,
			Yorke, Cole

*(Semi-Final, 2nd Leg – **Manchester United win 4-3 on aggregate**)*

FA CUP

Arsenal	D	0-0	

(Played at Villa Park, Birmingham)

Arsenal	W	2-1	Beckham
			Giggs

(After extra time – played at Villa Park, Birmingham)

Kings

" It was **absolutely fantastic** but that is what players like Ryan Giggs can do "

PETER SCHMEICHEL **after Giggs' wonder goal against Arsenal in the FA Cup**

DID YOU KNOW?

United have now won **ten FA Cup Semi-Finals** in a row, going back to 1976. The last one they lost was in 1970.

Simply unbelievable! The greatest month in the history of the club, or surely of any English club. **Three trophies won in the space of 11 days**. First the **Premiership**, which seemed to be slipping away after a draw at Liverpool, but Arsenal's defeat at Leeds meant a win over Spurs on the final day would be enough. After **David Beckham** equalised, **Andy Cole** grabbed the winner. Then the **FA Cup**, where **Teddy Sheringham**, on for the injured Roy Keane, proved his doubters wrong with the opening goal against Newcastle before **Paul Scholes** sealed the triumph. Then, amazingly, the **European Cup**. 1-0 down to Bayern Munich for most of the match, in a near replica of the Liverpool FA Cup game, a late equaliser from **Teddy** was followed by an injury-time winner from that most super of subs, **Ole Gunnar Solskjaer**. It really was **simply unbelievable!**

Three For

STATS

PREMIER LEAGUE

Aston Villa	W 2-1	Watson (o.g.) Beckham
Liverpool	D 2-2	Yorke, Irwin (pen)
Middlesbrough	W 1-0	Yorke
Blackburn Rovers	D 0-0	
Tottenham	W 2-1	Beckham, Cole

FA CUP

Newcastle Utd	W 2-0	Sheringham Scholes

(Final, Played at Wembley)

CHAMPIONS LEAGUE

Bayern Munich	W 2-1	Sheringham Solskjaer

(Final, Played at Nou Camp stadium, Barcelona)

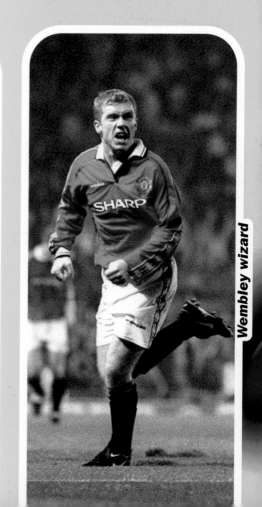

Wembley wizard

"Someone just had to do it"

OLE GUNNAR SOLSKJAER on his European Cup winning goal

Ah!

DID YOU KNOW?

Manchester United won the **European Cup Final** on what would have been the **90th birthday of Sir Matt Busby**, the manager of the side that won the competition in 1968.

Dwight Yorke

Few players have ever made so light of a club record price tag. The ever-smiling Dwight came from Aston Villa for over £12m, but scored goal after goal to propel United to their historic treble. His strikes against Inter Milan and Juventus stand out, along with the way he forged such a successful partnership with Andy Cole. Equal top of the Premiership scoring charts, Dwight looks like the biggest bargain for United since the purchase of Eric Cantona.

YOUNG PLAYER OF THE SEASON

Wes Brown

The young defender not only impressed for his club, but also for his country. When he made his England debut against Hungary in April, he had played fewer first team games than any previous England international. A player with a tremendous future.

PREMIER LEAGUE

DATE			Opponents	Home/Away	Result	Score	Attendance	Goalscorers
SAT	AUG	15	Leicester City	H	D	2-2	55,052	Sheringham, Beckham
SAT	AUG	22	West Ham United	A	D	0-0	26,039	
WED	SEP	9	Charlton Athletic	H	W	4-1	55,147	Solskjaer (2), Yorke (2)
SUN	SEP	12	Coventry City	H	W	2-0	55,193	Yorke, Johnsen
SUN	SEP	20	Arsenal	A	L	0-3	38,142	
SUN	SEP	24	Liverpool	H	W	2-0	55,181	Irwin, Scholes
SAT	OCT	3	Southampton	A	W	3-0	15,251	Yorke, Cole, Cruyff
SAT	OCT	17	Wimbledon	H	W	5-1	55,265	Cole (2), Giggs, Beckham, Yorke
SAT	OCT	24	Derby County	A	D	1-1	30,867	Cruyff
SAT	OCT	31	Everton	A	W	4-1	40,079	Yorke, Short (own goal), Cole, Blomqvist
SUN	NOV	8	Newcastle United	H	D	0-0	55,174	
SAT	NOV	14	Blackburn Rovers	H	W	3-2	55,198	Scholes (2), Yorke
SAT	NOV	21	Sheffield Wednesday	A	L	1-3	39,475	Cole
SUN	NOV	29	Leeds United	H	W	3-2	55,172	Solskjaer, Keane, Butt
SAT	DEC	5	Aston Villa	A	D	1-1	39,241	Scholes
SAT	DEC	12	Tottenham Hotspur	A	D	2-2	36,079	Solskjaer (2)
WED	DEC	16	Chelsea	H	D	1-1	55,159	Cole
SAT	DEC	19	Middlesbrough	H	L	2-3	55,152	Butt, Scholes
SAT	DEC	26	Nottingham Forest	H	W	3-0	55,216	Johnsen (2), Giggs
TUE	DEC	29	Chelsea	A	D	0-0	34,741	
SUN	JAN	10	West Ham United	H	W	4-1	55,180	Yorke, Cole (2), Solskjaer
SAT	JAN	16	Leicester City	A	W	6-2	22,091	Yorke (3), Cole (2), Stam
SUN	JAN	31	Charlton Athletic	A	W	1-0	20,043	Yorke
WED	FEB	3	Derby County	H	W	1-0	55,174	Yorke
SAT	FEB	6	Nottingham Forest	A	W	8-1	30,025	Yorke (2), Cole (2), Solskjaer (4)
WED	FEB	17	Arsenal	H	D	1-1	55,171	Cole
SAT	FEB	20	Coventry City	A	W	1-0	22,596	Giggs
SAT	FEB	27	Southampton	H	W	2-1	55,316	Keane, Yorke
SAT	MAR	13	Newcastle United	A	L	1-2	36,500	Cole (2)
SUN	MAR	21	Everton	H	W	1-3	55,182	Solskjaer, G Neville, Beckham
SAT	APR	3	Wimbledon	A	D	1-1	26,121	Beckham
SAT	APR	17	Sheffield Wednesday	H	W	3-0	55,270	Solskjaer, Sheringham, Scholes
SUN	APR	25	Leeds United	A	D	1-1	40,255	Cole
SAT	MAY	1	Aston Villa	H	W	2-1	55,189	Watson (own goal), Beckham
WED	MAY	5	Liverpool	A	D	2-2	44,702	Yorke, Irwin
SUN	MAY	9	Middlesbrough	A	W	1-0	34,665	Yorke
WED	MAY	12	Blackburn	A	D	0-0	30,436	
SUN	MAY	16	Tottenham Hotspur	H	W	2-1	55,189	Beckham, Cole

CHAMPIONS LEAGUE

DATE			Opponents	Home/Away	Result	Score	Attendance	Goalscorers
WED	AUG	12	LKS Lodz (2nd Qualifying, 1st leg)	H	W	2-0	55,000	Giggs, Cole
WED	AUG	26	LKS Lodz (2nd Qualifying, 2nd leg)	A	D	0-0	8,000	
			(Man United win 2-0 on aggregate)					
WED	SEP	16	Barcelona (Group D)	H	D	3-3	53,601	Giggs, Scholes, Beckham
WED	SEP	30	Bayern Munich (Group D)	A	D	2-2	53,000	Yorke, Scholes
WED	OCT	21	Brondby (Group D)	A	W	6-2	40,530	Giggs (2), Cole, Keane, Yorke, Solskjaer
WED	NOV	4	Brondy (Group D)	H	W	5-0	53,520	Beckham, Cole, P Neville, Yorke, Scholes
WED	NOV	25	Barcelona (Group D)	A	D	3-3	67,650	Yorke (2), Cole
WED	DEC	9	Bayern Munich (Group D)	H	D	1-1	54.434	Keane
WED	MAR	3	Inter Milan (Quarter-Final, 1st leg)	H	W	2-0	54,430	Yorke (2)
WED	MAR	17	Inter Milan (Quarter-Final, 2nd leg)	A	D	1-1	79,528	Scholes
			(Man United win 3-1 on aggregate)					
WED	APR	7	Juventus (Semi-final, 1st leg)	H	D	1-1	54,487	Giggs
WED	APR	21	Juventus (Semi-final, 2nd leg)	A	W	3-2	65,500	Keane, Yorke, Cole
			(Man United win 4-3 on aggregate)					
WED	MAY	26	Bayern Munich (Final)	Barcelona	W	2-1	90,000	Sheringham, Solskjaer

FA CUP

DATE			Opponents	Home/Away	Result	Score	Attendance	Goalscorers
SUN	JAN	3	Middlesbrough (3rd Round)	H	W	3-1	52,232	Cole, Irwin, Giggs
SUN	JAN	24	Liverpool (4th Round)	H	W	2-1	54,591	Yorke, Solskjaer
SUN	FEB	14	Fulham (5th Round)	H	W	1-0	54,798	Cole
SUN	MAR	7	Chelsea (Quarter-Final)	H	D	0-0	54,587	
WED	MAR	10	Chelsea (Replay)	A	W	2-0	33,075	Yorke (2)
SUN	APR	11	Arsenal (Semi-Final)	Villa Park	D	0-0	39,217	
WED	APR	14	Arsenal (Replay)	Villa Park	W	2-1	30,223	Beckham, Giggs
SAT	MAY	22	Newcastle United (Final)	Wembley	W	2-0	79.101	Sheringham, Scholes

WORTHINGTON CUP

DATE			Opponents	Home/Away	Result	Score	Attendance	Goalscorers
WED	OCT	28	Bury (3rd Round)	H	W	2-0	52,495	Solskjaer, Nevland
WED	NOV	11	Nottingham Forest (4th Round)	H	W	2-1	37,237	Solskjaer (2)
WED	DEC	2	Tottenham Hotspur (Quarter-Final)	A	L	1-3	35,702	Sheringham

CHARITY SHIELD

DATE			Opponents	Home/Away	Result	Score	Attendance	Goalscorers
SUN	AUG	9	Arsenal	Wembley	L	0-3	67,342	

FINAL RECKONING

You beauties!

UPS AND DOWNS

League position at the end of each month

FINAL TABLE

		P	W	D	L	F	A	Pts
1	**Man Utd**	**38**	**22**	**13**	**3**	**80**	**37**	**79**
2	Arsenal	38	22	12	4	59	17	78
3	Chelsea	38	20	15	3	57	30	75
4	Leeds	38	18	13	7	62	34	67
5	West Ham Utd	38	16	9	13	46	53	57
6	Aston Villa	38	15	10	13	51	46	55
7	Liverpool	38	15	9	14	68	49	54
8	Derby	38	13	13	12	40	45	52
9	Middlesbrough	38	12	15	11	48	54	51
10	Leicester	38	12	13	13	40	46	49
11	Tottenham	38	11	14	13	47	50	47
12	Sheff Wed	38	13	7	18	41	42	46
13	Newcastle	38	11	13	14	48	54	46
14	Everton	38	11	10	17	42	47	43
15	Coventry	38	11	9	18	39	51	42
16	Wimbledon	38	10	12	16	40	63	42
17	Southampton	38	11	8	19	37	64	41
18	Charlton	38	8	12	18	41	56	36
19	Blackburn	38	7	14	17	38	52	35
20	Nottm Forest	38	7	9	22	35	69	30

THAT'S PROGRESS?

	1997/98	1998/99
League position	2nd	1st
European competition	Quarter-Final (Champions Lg)	Final (Champions Lg)
FA Cup	Round 5	Final
League Cup	Round 3	Quarter-Final
Average attendance	55,168	55,188

BEST

Best Game

The **European Cup Final** in Barcelona against Bayern Munich. Maybe not the best performance, but the **most dramatic victory** in the history of the competition. **Sheer bliss**.

Best Signing

Dwight Yorke, though Jaap Stam was just behind. The Trinidadian edges it because – well, **we all love a goalscorer**. Absolutely brilliant.

Best Comeback

The **3-2 win over Juventus** in the Champions League, after the Italians took an early 2-0 lead that had everyone writing United off. **They should know better than that!**

Best Moment

When **Ole Gunnar Solskjaer** turned the ball over the line in Barcelona, three minutes into injury time, **to bring home the European Cup** after 31 years.

Worst Game

The **3-0 defeat at Arsenal** in September, marred by Nicky Butt's red card. As it was, the 1998 Premiership champions **couldn't last the pace** in the long run.

Worst Signing

United just don't make bad transfers! At a push, **Jesper Blomqvist** was the worst, but only because Jaap Stam and Dwight Yorke were so good.

Worst Collapse

The **2-2 draw at Liverpool**, after United had led 2-0. It gave Arsenal fleeting hope in the Premiership, and was a source of great joy to jealous Liverpool fans – **not that it mattered!**

Worst Moment

When **Bayern Munich took the lead** in the European Cup Final, to give a terrible start to such an important match. All's well that ends well!

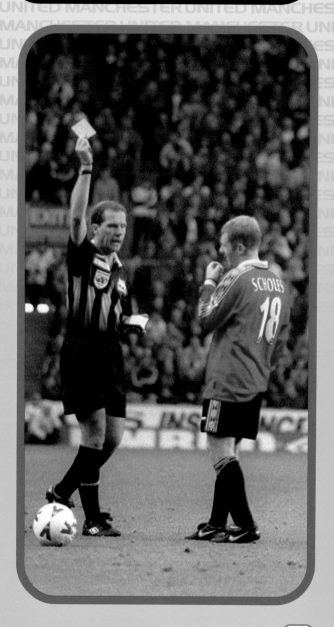

QUIZ

1 Which United player scored four goals in one match after coming on as a substitute?

2 How many years ago was it since United had won the European Cup?

3 **Which player** has been distorted by our artist in the picture to the right?

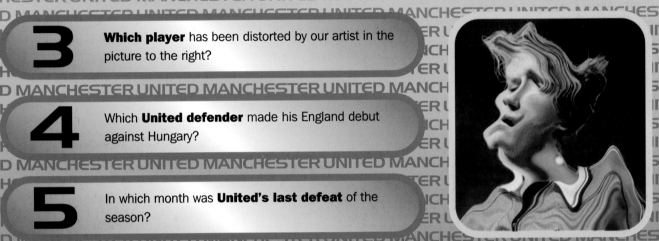

4 Which **United defender** made his England debut against Hungary?

5 In which month was **United's last defeat** of the season?

6 Which **European** opposition did United **hit for six**?

7 Which Premier League team **did United fail to beat** in any competition? Hard question, this.

8 Which former United player managed a side to victory at Old Trafford?

9 And which former United manager lost a home game 8-1 to the current side?

10 Finally, which team did the Treble?

Answers

1 Ole Gunnar Solskjaer **2** 31 **3** David Beckham **4** Wes Brown **5** December **6** Brondby **7** None! **8** Bryan Robson **9** Ron Atkinson **10** Manchester United, of course!